HOOK YOUR AUDIENCE

GW00715866

This book belongs t
Corporate Learning
&
Development

HOOK YOUR AUDIENCE

A collection of anecdotes, quips and quotations
providing a speaker's resource for trainers and managers

By Patrick Forsyth
Illustrations by Phil Hailstone

This edition published 2000

ISBN 1 870471 78 4

Published by:

Management Pocketbooks Ltd

14 East Street, Alresford, Hants SO24 9EE, U.K.

Tel: +44 (0)1962 735573   Fax: +44 (0)1962 733637

E-mail: pocketbks@aol.com

www.pocketbook.co.uk

Designed by:

ArtsFX Ltd., Unit 1, Barton Farm Industrial Estate, Chickenhall Lane,
Eastleigh, Hampshire SO50 6RP

Printed by:

Ashford Colour Press, Gosport, Hampshire, UK.

British Library Cataloguing-in-Publication Data –
A catalogue record for this book is available from the British Library.

CONTENTS

In praise of quotations

66 When a thing has been said and said well, have no scruple. Take it and copy it 99

Anatole France

66 I always have a quotation for everything – it saves original thinking 99

Dorothy L. Sayers

66 Next to being witty yourself, the best thing is to quote another's wit 99

Christian N. Bovee

66 An anthology is like all the plums and orange peel pulled out of a cake 99

Walter Raleigh

"A moment's insight is sometimes worth a life's experience"

Oliver Wendall Holmes

INTRODUCTION

" Where shall I begin, please, your Majesty?" he asked.
"Begin at the beginning," the King said gravely,
"and go on till you come to the end: then stop "
Lewis Carroll (Alice's Adventures in Wonderland)

This book and its purpose

Management was probably never easy. Certainly these days the pressures are considerable and many managers and executives might take the view that it can be downright difficult.

Success is only made likely by doing the right things and doing things right. Some of that consists of deploying perennial skills appropriately, indeed striving for excellence and taking a creative approach. Beyond that, one thing is for sure, we live in dynamic times. The pace of change has never been greater. Skills and approaches need developing and updating; new approaches need adding. Everything must be designed to bring about successful action which will generate the desired results. This whole process of ensuring change and adaptation is a current and ongoing challenge.

And challenge is the right word.

> 66 *There is always a well known solution to every human problem - neat, plausible ... and wrong* 99 H. L. Menkin

It is the job of managers and, in specific ways, of trainers, to prompt this process of update and change. In doing so they communicate ceaselessly. Hundreds – maybe thousands – of courses, conferences, meetings and briefings of all sorts are run every day, each dedicated to instigating some kind of change. Some are dire events, with reluctant participants cajoled along by those unwilling, unable or unprepared to make the event really useful.

Other events, the majority one hopes, are constructive and useful. They extend people's knowledge, help develop their skills and, longer term perhaps, change their attitudes. But there is no magic formula for making any of this happen.

Much of any success that is achieved is down to the style and conviction of the individual managers and trainers undertaking the task.

> 66 *People are persuaded more by the depth of your conviction than the height of your logic, more by your enthusiasm than by any proof you can offer* 99 Anon

Changing behaviour

Anyone communicating a message designed to instigate change carries a heavy responsibility. Their planning, preparation and, not least, their presentational skills all play a part. So does their ability to create involvement and prompt participation. This particular kind of communication is a skill that needs working at. It is not the intention here to instruct in training or presentational techniques, but rather to provide a resource to help augment in one particular way the level of skill deployed. A resource to help increase effectiveness in getting a message across, and – most important – getting it to stick.

It is well proven that any message is more likely to be given attention, credence and to be useful as a reference for the future, if it includes an element, beyond the message, that is memorable.

This includes something that sticks in the memory because it is particularly apt, clever, or amusing. Or something that is novel, that reminds people of things dear to them, paints a picture or encapsulates a concept or truth. All this with an economy of words and a homing in on the core message.

INTRODUCTION

In some ways we are talking about elements that might be regarded as embellishments or even digressions. But they can be disproportionately important. They act to turn what would otherwise be a perfectly workmanlike message, one that may or may not stick, into something with an added hook that makes its retention and use that much more likely.

This book contains a selection of such hooks. They include:
- Stories
- Quotations and quips
- Overheard remarks
- Proverbs, sayings and miscellaneous words of wit and wisdom

They may be classic, traditional, true, apocryphal, or invented. Some are composite, combining elements from several points. It does not matter. What does matter is that they work – they can lead into, exemplify or summarise a message and add something extra to it that makes it more likely to be effective.

" Repartee is what you wish you'd said " Heywood Broun

Using this book

There is no attempt at comprehensiveness here; given the content this would be impossible. The intention is to present a selection of items, and of forms, which together can act as a resource.

Some you may be able to use, as is. Others you may be able to adapt – changing, embellishing, extending or abbreviating them so that they better suit your purpose. Some you will have encountered before, doubtless in a variety of guises.

All can potentially enliven, embellish or add explanation to a meeting, conference or training session. Some may be best used to lead into a topic, others to summarise. Those included have been found useful by the author or by others, so what they may lack in originality they make up for by being, to an extent, road tested.

Some have a humorous feel, though not all are jokes in the *Here's a funny story* sense. Indeed humour is often more easily included with something other than a joke. Certainly it is safer to quote something pertinent to the point being made, which may also raise a smile. Going for, and failing to get, a big laugh can be difficult to pick up from without a hitch.

> 66 *If they like you, they don't applaud – they just let you live* 99 Bob Hope

INTRODUCTION

Arrangement

Few items are so tightly focused that they can be used only on a training session about, say, neurolinguistic programming. Many of the pieces have a multitude of potential topics around which they could be usefully quoted or used; and you may well be able to tweak them into further new applications. Yet any book needs some sort of structure. So the structure here aims to organise rather than exclude. Do not look only at one particular heading as you may miss something from elsewhere that might help you.

After some initial general points, the content has an arrangement which unashamedly rambles through the management process, and the groupings used simply mirror a variety of classic aspects of management and business. There is thus no intention to typecast anything. If you can use something in a way other than under its heading here then just do so.

Sources

Sometimes a source is clear (as with many quotations) and if so it is given. Often the original version of an item is lost in an impenetrable history of recycling and no source can be known with certainty, though I suppose all such words and phrases originated somewhere. Certainly the author claims no ownership for most of the entries and is grateful to all those who assisted with this compilation (see page 118). Feel free to continue the process of recycling.

We start with a story that can be used to break the ice and introduce any topic.

A new, smart, top of the range Volvo estate car, tow-bar on the back (for a boat, perhaps, or a horse-box) and all the extras, is being driven by a lady who appears to be from what might be referred to as the 'county set'. She is making a total mess of parking and is trying to get into the only remaining space in a busy town centre car park. The car goes to and fro varying the angle but failing to get it right. As it moves back from the space for the umpteenth time, the driver of a flashy little sports saloon (the kind with bolt on bumptiousness) who has been watching what has been going on, nips through the gap into the space.

The young man driving gets out and, as he locks the car, shouts out to the lady driver *"That's what you can do if you can drive properly, lady"*. Calmly and without pause, the lady slips the automatic gearbox into reverse, puts her foot on the accelerator and reverses hard into the other car. There is

a resounding crash and the tow-bar crushes the sports saloon in a shower of broken glass. In the silence following the crash, the lady presses the button to wind down the window and calls out: *"And that, young man, is what you can do if you have **money**"*.

And next we begin to look at what you can do if you have a good resource of quotations and anecdotes.

MANAGEMENT MAGIC

Managers and what they do

We start with some overall comments. What is management? It may be impossible to define. Though people try – some very personally:

> *Basically I try to jolly things along. After all, the problems can be solved by the people who have them. You have to try and coax them and love them into seeing ways in which they can help themselves* Management guru Sir John Harvey Jones

Some in a very down to earth way:

> *There is no magic in management. I make sure that people know what they are doing and then see that they do it* Bob Scholey (Chairman of British Steel)

The ultimate guru, Peter Drucker, says:

> *The basic task of management is to make people productive*

This seems solid enough, but this next thought is, for me, a little sad:

> 66 *Dreams have their place in managerial activity, but they need to be kept severely in check* 99 Lord Weinstock

In reality there is not just the management task to consider here, but also a two-way relationship between managers and their staff, illustrated thus:

> 66 *I don't want yes-men around me. I want everybody to tell the truth even if it costs them their job* 99
> Film producer Samuel Goldwyn

> 66 *You have to like the boss – if you don't he fires you* 99
> Overheard

It is easier to define what managers do. Six key tasks are certainly those of planning, organising, recruitment and selection, training and development, motivation, and control.

All contribute to the overall aim of achieving results through other people; ultimately such results usually have a financial component – such as producing a profit.

To do these things managers must consult, communicate, make decisions, solve problems, sit in important meetings –'Sorry, he can't be disturbed, he's in a meeting' – and build and develop their team.

66 *My manager's idea of consultation is saying 'When I want your opinion I'll give it you'* 99 Overheard

Communication is, of course, easy. This is usually attributed to the late Richard Nixon:

66 *I know that you understand what you think I said, but I am not sure you realize that what you heard is not what I meant* 99

It might be said of hundreds if not thousands of conversations taking place in offices around the world every day. Obviously none of us is personally anything other than crystal clear. If only!

Other regular tasks include decision making and problem solving.

> *When a person tells you 'I'll think it over and let you know' – you know* Olin Miller

> *One thing you can be certain of with my manager: her indecision is final* Overheard

> *There is no problem so big or complicated that it can't be run away from* Anon

> *A meeting is a gathering of important people who singly can do nothing, but together can decide that nothing can be done* Fred Allen

Important matters

For all its many facets, management is, of course, ultimately concerned not with mere tactics – but with weighty matters.

Once upon a time …… there was a wolf. He was scruffy, bedraggled and generally down at heel. He scratched a living where he could, but was regarded by the other animals as very low in the pecking order. He hated this; he wanted to be well-regarded and, after long fruitless hours trying to think how he could change his image, he concluded he needed help. He asked an aardvark, an anteater and an antelope for advice. Nothing; though the antelope suggested that he asked the lion, *"After all he's the king of the jungle"*. Risky it might be, but he was desperate, so he went and, very carefully, approached the lion, saying, *"I want people to like me, I don't want to be thought of as just a scruffy lowlife; I want to be loved. What can I do? Please advise me, your Majesty."*

The lion was irritated by the interruption, but he paused and gave it a moment's thought. *"You should become a bunny rabbit,"* said the lion, *"everyone loves a bunny rabbit, I think it's the long floppy ears and the big eyes. Yes, that's it - become a bunny rabbit."* The wolf did the wolf equivalent of touching his forelock, thanked the lion and slunk away. But almost at once he thought, *"Wait a minute, **how** do I become a bunny rabbit?"*

He went back, risked interrupting the lion again and said, *"Sorry ... excuse me, it is, of course, a wonderful idea of yours this business of my becoming a bunny rabbit, but ... but **how** exactly do I do that?"*

The lion drew himself up to his full height, ruffled his mane and said simply: *"As king of the jungle, I'm concerned with strategy – **how** you do it is for you to work out."*

Opportunities

As the proverb says:

> *There are no problems in life, only opportunities*

Though as another saying has it:

> *The trouble with opportunities is that they are so often disguised – as hard work*

> *A wise man will make more opportunities than he finds*
> Francis Bacon

So, whatever else managers must do, they must approach their tasks positively. Belief that you can succeed is half the battle.

> *I am a man of no convictions – at least I **think** I am*
> Christopher Hampton

Managers do not just cope with things as they occur. They have to initiate action, be innovative and make a positive difference. This can take time. Sometimes the length of time is an inherent part of the process.

After all, those producing tomorrow's newspaper have less time to act than those developing a new car. So, managers must be able to sustain their effort, take the long view and see things through, remaining optimistic throughout. The next page sets out what is perhaps the ultimate optimism story.

MANAGEMENT MAGIC

There is a tale from medieval times about a servant in the King's household who was condemned to life imprisonment for some small misdemeanour. Languishing in his cell, a thought struck him and he sent a message to the King promising that, if he were released, he would work day and night and, within a year, he would teach the King's favourite horse to talk.

TO BE OR NOT TO BE

This amused the King, and he ordered the servant to be released to work in the royal stables. The servant's friends were at once pleased to see him released, yet frightened for him too; after all horses do not talk, however much training they get. *"What will you do?"*, they all asked. *"So much can happen in a year,"* he replied. *"I may die, the King may die, or – who knows – the horse may talk!"*

Who knows indeed; I for one hope that by the time the year was up he had thought of another ruse.

On the other hand, remember:

> 66 *Things are going to get a lot worse before they get worse* 99
> Lily Tomlin

Reasons for non-achievement

So far, so good. But now – optimistic or not – management must bear in mind that the ubiquitous Murphy's Laws mean that everything is pretty much impossible anyway. So, pausing to list a ten-point interpretation of these classic laws, we will move on to examine some specific areas of the manager's job in more detail.

Murphy's Laws

1. If anything can go wrong, it will

2. Nothing is ever as simple as it seems

3. If you mess with something for long enough, it will break

4. Nothing ever works out exactly as you expect

5. Whatever you want to do, there is always something else you have to do first

6. If you try to please everybody, **somebody** won't like it

7. If you explain something so that no one could possibly misunderstand, someone will

8. If everything is going according to plan, then it's a sure sign that something is about to go wrong

9. Nothing is certain until it has happened (and even when you think it has – double check)

10. The only predictable thing about your day is that something totally unexpected will happen.

To this list, perhaps we should add the proviso that if a computer is involved you should multiply the likelihood of any disaster striking by two, three or even more.

FIRST THINGS FIRST

Purposeful planning

Before managers do anything, they must plan.   Well they should, though there are doubtless many subordinates who would swear that their managers make it up as they go along; sometimes with no great imagination.

The saying, 'Plan the work, and work the plan' is just a saying, but every management guru worth their salt has a version of the thought, applicable to organisations, departments or whatever.

> *If you don't know where you are going, any road will do*

Peter Drucker perhaps first voiced it in those words; the original goes back much further and makes the point with considerably more style.

> *Would you tell me, please, which way I ought to go from here?"*
> *"That depends a good deal on where you want to get to," said the Cat.*
> *"I don't much care where ... " said Alice.*
> *"Then it doesn't matter which way you go," said the Cat.*
> *" ... so long as I get **somewhere**," Alice added as an explanation.*
> *"Oh, you're sure to do that," said the Cat, "if only you walk long enough*
>
> Lewis Carrol (Alice in Wonderland)

Pachydermatous planning

It is said that planning is rather like making love to an elephant.

The elephant doesn't feel it, you don't like it, the main activity is at a high level but everything gets trampled underfoot, nothing happens for two years – and then - all hell breaks loose!

Life is what happens while you are making other plans
John Lennon

Right on target

> 66 *In this company, planning is no more than anticipating the inevitable, and then taking the credit for it* 99 Overheard

The following classic tale makes a similar point:

A medieval King is crossing the forest with his entourage on a hunting trip. On a series of trees they see a painted target and in the exact centre of each there is an arrow. *"What incredible accuracy,"* says the King, *"we must find the archer."*

Further on they catch up with a small boy carrying a bow and arrow. He is frightened at being stopped by the King's party, but admits that he fired the arrows. *"You did shoot the arrows, didn't you?"* queries the King, *"you didn't just stick them into the targets by hand?"* The boy replies, *"Your majesty, I swear I shot all the arrows from a hundred paces."* *"Incredible,"* says the King, *"you must accept a job at the palace, I must have an archer of such brilliance near me. But tell me, you are so young, how do you achieve such accuracy?"*

The boy looks sheepish: "*Well,*" he says, "*first I step out a hundred paces, then I fire the arrow into the tree... and then I walk back and paint the target on the tree.*"

CREATING ORDER OUT OF CHAOS

Organising for action

People have probably always needed to be organised. Even early man, setting up the first axehead producing cooperative must have found out pretty quickly that someone needed to be in charge and that someone else needed to head up marketing, production ('Stonemaker' or 'Stone production facilitating executive'?), and so on. And that each person in turn needed to organise their particular bit: eg: marketing setting up a 'Free mammoth pie when you buy three axeheads' offer and deploying a team to carve signs advertising this on strategic rocks. They might even have thought up a brandname: Axeheads R Us, perhaps.

Early quotes about organisation do not seem dated:

> 66 *First organise the near at hand, then organise the far removed.*
> *First organise the inner, then organise the outer. First organise the*
> *basic, then organise the derivative. First organise the strong, then*
> *organise the weak. First organise the great, then organise the*
> *small. First organise yourself, then organise others* 99
>
> Zhuge Liang (a Chinese general who wrote that in the 2nd century AD)

Of course, everything might be pre-organised for you, as in the next story.

Management succession

A newly appointed manager comes into his new office for the first time and sees three crisp, white envelopes on the otherwise empty desk. They are numbered one to three, and each is addressed to him by name and indicates it is from his predecessor in the job. Each has one single sentence on it – *If you have a problem open first envelope, if you have another problem open the second and similarly the third.*

Almost immediately a problem crops up. The new manager, grateful to his predecessor, opens the first envelope. On the white card inside is printed: *Whatever the problem blame your predecessor.* He does and it gets him off the hook, but another problem soon occurs. He opens the second envelope and reads a card which says: *Reorganise the department.* He does just that, in the process giving someone else the task of sorting out the problem.

But a third problem follows quickly on the heels of the others. Encouraged by his experience to date and the helpful line taken by his predecessor, he opens the third envelope.

The card inside says simply: *Prepare three white envelopes.*

CREATING ORDER OUT OF CHAOS

One of the skills of management planning is concerned with matching people's skills to the tasks that must be tackled.

A university professor was quizzing a group of students about a task set for them during a field study trip. They had been asked to ascertain the height of a local church tower, and the only tool they could use was a barometer.

The engineering student could only say it was about 200 feet high. He had dropped the barometer from the top of the tower and done a calculation based on how long it took to hit the ground. The mathematics student had measured the length of the barometer, measured the distance from the top of the tower to where the line of sight hit the ground, calculated various angles and triangles and reckoned the tower was 198 feet high.

The business student was completely confident: "*I know exactly how high it is,*" he said. "*How did you work that out?*" asked the professor. He explained that he had taken a different approach from his colleagues. "*When I went into the churchyard I saw the Vicar going into the church,*" he said. "*I told him that if he knew and could tell me the height of the church tower, I would give him the barometer. And he said it was 199 feet and 6 inches.*"

ROUND PEGS IN ROUND HOLES

Finding the right people

Before managers can do anything very much they have to assemble their teams. This is, of course, easy, primarily because it is well known that just having the title 'Manager' bestows on you infallible people-judging abilities. (If you believe this you are in trouble, but a prime candidate for being sold Tower Bridge.) In fact, finding the right people is a skill; recruitment and selection need to be carried out carefully and systematically.

Having the right people in place creates a fundamental basis for success. Nothing is worse than finding that a group comprises people who can only be categorised as not competent enough to keep, yet not sufficiently incompetent to fire.

" They said they had half a mind to go into management, but they were obviously way overqualified " Overheard

" Hire the person who can do the job – and accept that they aren't necessarily the person you want to be best friends with " Mark McCormack

I know what I want

The M.D. sat in on all the interviews with applicants for the job of new financial controller, though he took no active part. Nevertheless, at the end of each interview the Personnel Director always politely asked whether there were any additional questions he wished to ask the applicant, and each time the M.D. asked just one, "*Please tell me what is the answer to 2 + 2?*". He did not react to the puzzled expressions as each candidate answered "*4*". Finally he spoke again, "*You're hired,*" he said to the final candidate who had answered his question with another – "*What do you want it to be?*".

Note: another version of this kind of story has the applicant giving an answer which is not quite correct and being told she is hired because 'you were closest to the right answer'.

> 66 *You're an appallingly dull fellow, unimaginative, timid, spineless, easily dominated, no sense of humour, tedious company and irrepressibly drab and awful. And, whereas in most professions these would be considered drawbacks, in accountancy they are a positive boon* 99
> From the radio programme: *And now for something completely different*

66 *There is a world of difference between a good sound candidate, and a candidate who sounds good* 99 Anon

66 *Recruitment is easy. Find and appoint a good candidate. Watch and wait to see if they perform satisfactorily. If their performance proves unacceptable – don't appoint them* 99
Overheard

At the time when BandAid was raising money for the famine in Africa, versions of the following story enjoyed some currency:

God decides that some divine help is called for to help relieve the starvation. He rejects the idea of miracles and instead resolves to seek out an agent on Earth to act on his behalf. He picks a house at random and sends an Angel to recruit a helper. The Angel rings the front door bell and waits. After a while the door opens to reveal the now familiar figure of Bob Geldof. His hair is wild and he looks as if he has just got out of bed and has proceeded to the door by going backwards through a hedge. This is, apparently, the person God has chosen to orchestrate a mammoth fundraising exercise and prompt an aid programme of unprecedented proportions.

The Angel – unconvinced – hesitates, then asks: *"Is anyone else in?"*

A LITTLE LEARNING

Developing the skills that create success

Dynamic times and the pressure of change make training an ongoing process in most organisations. People need to keep up to date and they also need to extend existing skills and cultivate new skills. Often this is the result of outside changes in markets and amongst competing organisations. So, in the words of the old saying: *If you think training is expensive, try ignorance.*

Trainers clearly believe training is a 'good thing', and their expertise is, of course, legendary (How many trainers does it take to change a light bulb? None, they form one syndicate to take the old one out and another to put the new one in. Or: One, but in that case the lightbulb must really want to be changed.)

> (On attitudes to training) 66 *What if I train my staff and they leave?*" The only response to which is: "*What if you don't train them – and they stay?* 99

At worst training is verbal Mogadon, at best it is something people see as an important resource and one that makes a real difference to the organisation and its people.

> 66 *It is what you learn after you know it all that counts* 99
> John Wooden

❝ For goodness sake, don't ask me if you can go on an assertiveness training course – just go and register ❞ Overheard

❝ John's results are simply not good enough. They are a disgrace to both of us – I'll have to try harder ❞ Overheard

❝ Training? In my company training is all wings and no feet ❞ Overheard

The best training bridges the gap between theory and practice.

❝ I hear and I forget, I see and I remember, I do and I understand ❞

Training can impart knowledge, develop skills and (longer term) change attitudes. It is not always a comfortable process:

❝ Change is made not without inconvenience, even from worse to better ❞ Richard Hooker

❝ Knowledge advances by steps, and not by leaps ❞ Lord Macaulay

A LITTLE LEARNING

The impossible takes a little longer

Sometimes a new skill may feel too difficult to acquire. If this is coupled with scepticism about its usefulness (something the author remembers feeling once about acquiring keyboard skills) then learning may be stillborn.

The following story makes a good point.

An American college student is going on an exchange visit, swapping with a student from a small town in northern Thailand. After much planning and preparation, and with some apprehension, she sets off on the long journey. After an international flight and a domestic flight, she is sitting in a car with her host travelling the final leg to the town where she will spend a year of her life.

She expresses her fears about the language, Thai being a notoriously difficult language to learn. Her host reassures her that she will manage it without difficulty, but, unconvinced, she is disbelieving. *"It will surely not be difficult,"* he says. *"No one in your host family speaks English. You have no choice; you will learn to speak Thai."* *

If it is essential, many things can be achieved. Accepting that it is essential may be the first step.

* The full story is told in the book Touch the Dragon by Karen Connelly (Black Swan)

Memorandum

FROM ~~TO~~: ~~All Managers~~ SAM WHITE

TO ~~FROM~~: Training Manager

Future training

A series of workshops is being scheduled on the important topic of delegation. You are nominated for this and should attend on 15 December. The event will be in Conference Room B from 9-30 until 4-30.

More details will be circulated later, meantime make sure the date goes in your diary.

PLEASE NOTE THAT I CANNOT ATTEND ON THIS DAY BUT I WILL SEND MY ASSISTANT.

Real life

Some anecdotes can be drawn from real training events and actual course delegates. For example:

◆ On one course (on presentation skills) video recording equipment was being used to record and critique delegates' performance. At lunchtime – the event was in a hotel meeting room – the group went off to the restaurant. When they returned the trainer found that someone had stolen the video camera. As they hurriedly organised a replacement it was noticed that the camera and recorder had been left running on 'record' over lunch. The video showed a clear picture of the thief entering the room and taking the camera.

The local police recognised him and the camera was recovered before the group took their afternoon break.

- To put people at their ease and stress the acceptability of an informal atmosphere, I recall and quote the time a participant hobbled into a public seminar. He explained that he had hurt his back, produced a cushion for his head and lay full length in the open U-shape layout for two days! No one minded, indeed it helped create the right atmosphere.

Most trainers have many such experiences and it is perhaps worth keeping a note of them.

Now, as a final word linked to training, another quotation:

> 66 *In theory there is no difference between theory and practice. In practice there is* 99   Yogi Berra

PROVIDING THE CARROTS

Motivating to create positive attitudes

A U.S. Army manual from the last century listed various rules for directing the mules that were used to carry supplies. The first was simple: *strike the mule between the eyes with a stout stick.*

Donkeys are better encouraged with carrots than with sticks, so too motivation is an essential element of good management. It is well proven that performance is better when people's motivation is high. But, like so much else in management, it does not just happen. Creating a positive motivational climate needs working at. Every aspect of the management task will affect people and influence how they feel about their organisations, their managers, their work and more. Throughout their activities, managers must continuously keep in mind the need to motivate. Any action taken should be carefully considered, and given some time to be effective.

Managers must use all possible avenues to enhance people's feelings. It is also helpful to understand the way motivation works and the complexities it involves.

66 Nothing is ever achieved without enthusiasm 99 R. W. Emerson

66 Only in bad novels do people do things for one reason 99
Peter Carey

The same level of attention should be given to major incentive schemes involving large numbers of people and to the small, day to day things that play an equal part in the overall process.

66 Sometimes the most effective motivation is just to say 'thank you' 99 Zig Ziglar

PROVIDING THE CARROTS

A question of perception

A man goes to visit a jail. He tours the cells and then goes outside where, close by the prison, inmates are employed breaking rocks from a small quarry. He is allowed to talk to some of the prisoners and asks how they survive the harsh regime. Most are dispirited and despondent. They describe their existence and their work as hard, interminable and boring.

Just one takes a different view. He says that he enjoys getting out and working away from the prison building. *"It cheers me up,"* he says. *"I imagine the end result – I'm playing a key part in building a cathedral."*

If all else fails you in your attempts to motivate people, then a little good old fashioned flattery may work for you. This is something that must be directed with care. Most people are sophisticated, they see flattery coming a mile away and it may well be self-defeating (and if you have just said, *"Quite right, if my manager flattered me I wouldn't be taken in for a moment"* – then you have just been influenced by flattery yourself!).

> 66 *The greatest discovery of my generation is that a human being can alter his life by altering his attitude of mind* 99 William James

MAKING IT STICK

Management control

Even the best laid plans and the most carefully organised people need some element of control. Control is no more than identifying variances, measuring what we intended to happen against what has actually happened and seeing if there is a difference. If results are better than the intention then we hold a celebratory party.   (Actually we should still look to see what can be learned from it and how that might affect future performance.)

If results are worse than expected then we need to instigate contingency plans. Sometimes this involves the merest nudge on the tiller.   Sometimes the action must be drastic – fire whoever is failing or re-organise the department concerned.

> *In this company they use the ultimate control. It's called 'Planned insecurity' – every month whoever is doing least well is fired!* Overheard

> *If everything is going well, then you do not know what is going on* Anon

Really it is

On the principle that all rules are meant to be broken, controls are meant to be circumvented. Indeed much time is expended in many an organisation by people arranging things so that what they have done is more difficult to check up on. They disguise the facts or construct strategically placed smoke screens around their activities.

Then the simplest things may not be what they seem. Take people's expenses; the amount of money claimed back from the organisation to cover costs incurred in the pursuit of business activities. This is sometimes referred to cynically (or realistically?) as the 'swindle sheet'. I cannot trace the source, but I remember being quoted the following long ago:

In Brighton she was Brenda,
She was Patsy up in Perth,
In Cambridge she was Candina
The sweetest girl on Earth.
In Stafford she was Stella,
The pick of all the bunch,
But down in his expenses,
She was Petrol, Oil and Lunch.

GETTING THE MESSAGE ACROSS

The ins and outs of communication

Communication is basically essential to achieving cognition in the workplace, and creating a situation in which people can operate in a way that reflects the appropriate information, and makes possible the achievement of certain agreed objectives.

You may well say "*What?*".

Start again: Communication must be clear to enable people to produce the right result.

Better.

Communication is something else that suffers from the strongly-held belief that it is easy. It must be clear, yet is easily (and often) not. People must listen and often do not. The communicator must take responsibility for what they put over, and yet, often, exchanges end with someone saying something like *"What's the matter with this idiot, doesn't he understand anything?"*, when they perhaps should be asking themselves: *"Did I explain that as well as I could?"*.

> **❝** *The ability to express an idea is almost as important as the idea itself* **❞** Bernard Baruch

The dangers of assumption

It is said that you should never assume anything: *assumption makes an 'ass out of u and me'.* All sorts of things act to dilute the effectiveness of communication, everything from prejudice to the lack of a clear frame of reference. Assumption is a particular danger, as the next anecdote illustrates:

The pompous Chairman of a large, traditional City institution once entered the lift with two important visitors and observed a young man smoking, in what was part of a strictly controlled non-smoking environment. Furious, he asked the young man how much he earned in a week. When he had been told a figure, he reached into his pocket, produced his wallet and peeled off the appropriate amount of money. He handed it over to the young man saying: *"You are smoking in a non-smoking area and in this organisation that is simply not acceptable. You're fired. Go to Personnel and tell them"* – he gave his name – *"that I sent you to collect your cards."*

The young man did not reply. He got out at the next floor, dutifully delivered his message, left the building and – happily – returned to the courier company for which he worked with the money safely in his pocket.

Focus on others

Communication is not simply something we do to other people, it is an interaction that takes place between people – the good communicator thinks about both sides of this transaction.

> **❝** *I guess I should warn you. If I turn out to be particularly clear, you've probably misunderstood what I've said* **❞**
> Dr. Alan Greenspan

Successful communication most often comes from the old expedient of *engaging the brain before the mouth* and directing the message in a way that respects both the other party and the inherent difficulties of communication.

> **❝** *I am not arguing with you – I am telling you* **❞** James Whistler

> **❝** *When I am getting ready to reason with a man, I spend one third of my time thinking about myself and what I am going to say; and two thirds thinking about him and what he is going to say* **❞**
> Abraham Lincoln

Wrong!

Stories abound of communication failing in some way. The following is a classic:

Who said that?

It is a dark and stormy night. The Captain of a ship, peering ahead from the bridge, suddenly sees a light dead ahead and, to avoid a collision, he sends a signal: *"Change your course 10 degrees west"*.

The reply comes back: *"Change your course, 10 degrees east,"* and angrily the Captain sends back, *"I'm a navy captain, change your course"*.

"I'm only a seaman, but change your course now, Sir," comes back the reply.

Furious now, the Captain shouts into the radio: *"This is one of Her Majesty's battleships, give way at once,"* but hears a final response: *"This is a lighthouse. Your move."*

Even with care, to an extent we take a risk every time we communicate; yet without communication, management and organisations would barely exist.

> 66 *To escape criticism – do nothing, say nothing, be nothing* 99
> Elbert Hubbard

Just plain silly ....

Sometimes communication is so misjudged as to be a nonsense. Examples abound (you may well know, or collect, more). The following give the flavour:

- Note to milkman: *Please leave two pints. If note should blow away – please ring bell*
- A cable sent by a journalist to Hollywood said simply: *How old Cary Grant?* The reply came back promptly: *Old Cary Grant fine, how are you?*
- *Blackcurrant juice drink comes in two flavours: Orange and Strawberry* (soft drinks label)
- *Permanent markers, with eraser* (on marker pen pack)
- *Subtitles will begin shortly* (Subtitle on BBC Tomorrow's World)
- *... and an insurance policy for dead people* (benefits listed in staff manual)
- *What do you think of the government's record?* (Mori poll question – which produced inappropriate answers that included: *I didn't know they were in the hit parade)*
- *Please remove all clothing before giving this item to a child* (warning notice on teddy bear)

And finally a wonderful announcement from an airline pilot explaining a long delay to weary passengers:

Poor communication can cause small problems – or complete communications breakdowns.

Now listen up

Listening effectively is a skill. It is an inherent part of an overall capability in communications, and something that staff very much appreciate in their managers.

> ❝ *My manager always says 'You can speak to me any time. I have an open door policy' – trouble is they are never behind it* ❞
> Overheard

> ❝ *It is a rare person who wants to hear what he doesn't want to hear* ❞ Dick Cavett

In can be useful to point out to people how the focus of our listening varies (or fails). For example, everyone can identify with the feeling of listening, disagreeing, and then spending the remaining time mentally composing a response or denial – rather than listening.

You can also use a teaser to make the point, for example saying to people: *"Help me out here, I can't think of the word, what's that special writing called – in the form of little bumps on the page representing the letters, the thing deaf people run their fingers over to help them read?"* Most people will say "Braille", having not heard clearly that what was said is nonsense: in fact, it is blind people who use Braille.

There are many versions of this kind of teaser; more can be collected.

ON YOUR FEET

The ability to make a good formal 'on your feet' presentation is not optional for most people in an organisational environment, it is a core skill; the absence of which can potentially have many adverse effects.

> *The human brain starts working the moment you are born and never stops until you stand up to speak in public*
> Sir George Jessel

There are those who know the feeling, described above, all too well.

> (Chairman to after dinner speaker) *Are you going to speak now, or shall we let them enjoy themselves a bit longer?* Overheard

It is because of the potential difficulty, and the fact that by no means all presentations are as good as they might be, that this area provides a significant opportunity for many people. Ensure that you can make a good presentation and you give yourself an advantage. Ensure you can do something noticeably above average and that advantage gives you a major edge.

As a character says in the Video Arts training film on the subject, entitled 'I wasn't prepared for that,' a presentation is "... *the business equivalent of an open goal*".

Most people, even the more experienced, are nervous of presentational situations. It is not nerves, as one wag said, but 'creative apprehension'.

"*If you are not nervous,*" a man, the keynote conference speaker, was asked by a woman just before going through to the conference room, "*what are you doing in the 'Ladies'?*". And indeed the adrenalin that is produced 'on the day' is often felt to help make all go well.

Presentation needs care and most people cannot just 'wing it' – as the following anecdote makes all too clear.

Beware of operating on 'automatic pilot'

A true story that involves a presentation (or illustrates the general need to think first):

A firm of architects had been seeking what looked like a profitable brief to build residential training centres for a large charity. They attended meetings, made suggestions, produced designs, plans and costings. Finally, successfully short-listed, they are asked to make a presentation to the charity's governing committee.

With a tight deadline, the team prepare – in haste amidst other projects and pressures. Three people will speak. They are used to working together, and meet only briefly, deciding rapidly who will take which role. They are used to using sophisticated visual aids, and prepare slides to illustrate their designs. They have arranged how long each speaker will take and leave for the meeting feeling that, although they have not had a full rehearsal, they are well prepared to make a good impression on the committee.

Arriving at the charity's offices in good time, they are shown to the meeting room and one of them asks where the power point is so that they can set up their projector. The secretary showing them in looks startled. "*Why?*" she says. "*You must know that most of the committee members are blind.*" Despite the fact that they are in the headquarters of a major charity for the blind no one had thought of it – after all "*presentations automatically mean slides*".

Two minutes later they began their presentation with the expensively made slides hidden away. Their planned approach was, in the event, not appropriate and the impression given was less than professional.

They did not get the work.

(But for a long time afterwards preparation for presentations was more thorough!)

> 66 *The golden rule for all presenters is to imagine that you are in the audience* 99 David Martin

WRITE RIGHT

Predictions of the 'paperless office' have proved wildly over-optimistic. Paper continues to breed in the warm environment of the average office like the proverbial rabbit. But how much of it is useful? Too much business writing is executed on automatic pilot, with no real thought. What comes out the other end can be awash with sequipedalians (an appropriately long word for long words; incidentally, why is abbreviated such a long word?) or, at worst, a combination of gobbledygook and officespeak. Like the ability to make good presentations, the ability to execute good, memorable, and understandable business writing is a real 'career skill'. And a skill that not only helps get the job done, but ensures the writer is seen in a positive light.

> 66 *Writing is easy; all you do is sit staring at a blank sheet of paper until the drops of blood form on your forehead* 99
> Gene Fowler

Although the above was doubtless said about a more creative kind of writing than that needed in business, this will ring true with many people.

The document on the next page, seen on a company notice board, is complete with subtitles. It may be exaggerated, but makes a good point about dense style.

Progress report

During the survey period that ended on 14 February, considerable progress
has been made in the preliminary work directed towards the establishment of
initial activities. *(We are getting ready to start, but we have not done
so yet.)* The background information has been surveyed and the
functional structure of the component parts of the cognizant
organisation has been clarified. *(We have looked at what
needs to be done, and decided George should do it.)*

Considerable difficulty has been encountered in the
selection of optimum approaches and methods, but this
problem is being attacked vigorously and we expect the
development phase will proceed satisfactorily. *(George is
working out what exactly to do.)* In order to prevent
unnecessary duplication of previous efforts in
related fields, it was necessary to establish a
survey project which has comprised of a
rather extensive tour around various
departments with immediate access to
the system. *(George has visited everyone
and drunk a lot of coffee.)*

GEORGE

Continued...

The Steering Committee held its regular meeting and considered several important policy matters appertaining to the overall organisational levels of the line and staff responsibilities that devolve on the personnel associated with the specific assignments resulting from the broad functional specifications laid down. *(What?)* It is believed that the rate of progress will continue to accelerate as necessary personnel are made available for the necessary operational discussions. *(When George finds someone who knows what to do, matters will move forward.)*

——————————— ▪ ———————————

❝ I never write metropolis when I get paid the same money to write city ❞ Mark Twain

An eye on language

Here is an interesting teaser which can be used when discussing anything to do with language (it makes a good exercise for early arrivals at a meeting to occupy themselves with before the start). Ask people to read the following passage and answer the conundrum it presents.

As you scan this short paragraph, try to spot what is unusual about it. Half an hour is normal for many to find a clarification which is logical and satisfactory; or you may find an instant solution. I do not say that anything is wrong about it, simply that it is unusual. You may want to study its grammatical construction to find a solution, but that is not a basis of its abnormality, nor is its lack of any information, logical points or conclusion. If you work in communications you may find that an aid to solving this particular conundrum. It is not about anagrams, synonyms, antonyms or acrostics – but it *is* unusual. Why?

Note: the answer is printed, upside-down on a piece of paper stuck under the publisher's chair in Alresford. Sorry; actually it is on page 65.

WRITE RIGHT

Getting it right

Any consideration of business writing should include the injunction to edit carefully what has been written. Few of us write text we are wholly satisfied with first time, and editing is a necessary part of the drafting of most documents. This point can be introduced or reinforced with a story from the musical world.

A now famous operatic singer was invited to perform at a major gala concert in Italy, something that was a wonderful opportunity very early in his career. He was thrilled to be there and flattered to find that, having sung his particular aria, he was called back for several encores. He said as much to the stage manager as he pushed him out onto stage again for the fourth time. "*No, no, Senor,*" he was told, "*I am afraid they will ask you to sing it again and again – until you get it right!*"

> ❝ *I was working on the proof of one of my poems all the morning, and took out a comma. In the afternoon I put it back again* ❞ Oscar Wilde

Correct

Once fine-tuning is complete and the writer is satisfied with what is written, the final check is simply for accuracy. Spelling is a problem for some, and there is not a spell checker made that will catch everything.

Eye have this knew spell chequer witch came with my PC
Eye trussed it two do its job hand cheque this poem four me.
It plainly marked fore my revue miss stakes I did not sea
So now I'm shore yawl be pleased to no
It's letter-perfect inn it's weigh
Course my spell chequer tolled me sew.

So, please note: we can knot all ways trussed hour word processors (sic).

Similarly, one feels for the author of a computer manual which had a bold, boxed, statement on an early page which read "*THIS MANUAL HAS BEEN CAREFULLY TO AVOID ERRORS*".

You have been warned.

(Note: the answer to the teaser on page 63 is that it is written without using the commonest letter in the English language: the "e".)

WRITE RIGHT

The reader reacts

At the end of the day, any piece of business writing is judged by its readers, and particularly by their actions. Write a report designed to persuade people to *do something*, even something as simple as attending a meeting, and you automatically put yourself in a position to see the results. So, come the moment, if you find yourself sitting in the meeting room all on your own you may perhaps judge that your writing did not get your message across.

There is a story of an important report circulating around a large organisation. On the front of the report is stapled a slip with a long list of names of those who need to read it. As it is passed on down the list, with names being ticked off, comments are added. One of the recipients takes a profound dislike to the document and, as he reads it, disagrees completely with one particular section. In disgust he scribbles the word 'Balls!' in the margin. However, thinking of the status of subsequent readers and the possible offence this might cause, he rubs it out and substitutes the phrase 'Round objects'.

A week later the report arrives back with its originator. In the margin the comment 'Round objects' remains. Underneath it in a second hand is written: 'Who is this Round, and why does he object?'.

GETTING TOGETHER

The gentle art of meetings

Most people have a memory of coming out of some dire and interminable meeting muttering 'What a complete waste of time!' For some it is a recent or regular memory. Often such feelings are justified. Meetings must have clear objectives, the right people must attend (and *not* attend), and there must be an agenda. Timing is important (do any business meetings start on time?) and so too is how a meeting is chaired.

Good meetings can be effective. Issues can be constructively debated, decisions prompted and a creative element brought to bear over and above the way an individual would deal with something.

    66 *Meetings … are rather like cocktail parties. You don't want to go, but you're cross not to be asked* 99 Jilly Cooper

    66 *Meetings are indispensable when you don't want to do anything* 99 J. K. Galbraith

    66 *The appointment of the unfit and unwilling to do the unnecessary* 99 Sir David Davenport-Han

No wonder many people consider that the ideal meeting is attended by two
people … one of whom is absent!

GETTING TOGETHER

Here's a story about teamworking at its least convincing.

An in-company training programme was taking place where the full senior management team were all attending as a group. One of the key objectives of the session was the need for them to practise and develop teamwork.

As the time went by, the arguments and disagreements grew and intensified. If the Production Manager made a comment, then the Accountant derided it. If the Marketing Manager made a suggestion then the Head of Research contradicted it. On the first afternoon the group split into syndicates and the factions divided and argued more, with even the suggestion as to who might chair one group prompting seemingly endless disagreement.

The trainer worked hard to pour oil on troubled waters. Finally, towards the end of the day, her patient facilitating gave way to an outburst. As the Marketing Manager and the Production Manager went at each other like unruly kids in the playground, she banged the table and shouted: *"Is there nothing you two can agree on?"*. There was a shocked silence for a few seconds. The two looked at each other, then said – in unison – *"Well, neither of us ever agrees with the Accountant!"*.

In reality, of course, meetings must be effective and result in decisions made and action taken. That, in turn, means that people must work constructively, and better still creatively, together.

> 66 *The boat won't go, if we all don't row* 99   Harvey Mackay

Definition: *A committee is a meeting which keeps minutes and wastes hours.*

HAVE I GOT YOU WHERE YOU WANT ME?

Negotiating a deal

Negotiation follows, and goes hand in hand with, persuasive communication (or selling). Selling persuades people to take some action; negotiation agrees the terms and conditions on which a deal is done. On the one hand it is unashamedly adversarial. On the other, both parties must be satisfied or no deal will be done: the so-called 'win-win' outcome.

> " Throwing an eleven foot rope to someone drowning twenty feet from the riverbank is more than meeting him halfway "
> Lenny Bruce

> " You don't get what you deserve, you get what you negotiate " Anon

Definition: The process during which the fine print is a clause for concern.

The to and fro rituals of negotiation must be allowed to take place, the techniques must be understood and utilised appropriately and sufficient time taken to make a deal. And throughout, one must be watchful.

> " When a man tells me he's going to put all his cards on the table, I always look up his sleeve " Lord Hore-Belisha

The very first negotiation

Key to negotiation is the concept of trading concessions, the to and fro process that balances what each party gives or takes and ultimately dictates the outcome, as this story makes clear:

In the Garden of Eden Adam is comfortable but lonely. He calls out to God telling him how he feels and God's voice replies from the heavens: *"I have the perfect solution for you, I can create 'woman' for you."*. Adam is pleased to hear there is a solution, but asks: *"What's a woman, Lord?"*

"Woman will be my greatest creation," says God, *"she will be intelligent, caring, sensitive, and her beauty will surpass anything on Earth. She will understand your every mood, care for you in every way, and she will make you happier than you can imagine. She will be a perfect partner for you. But there will be a cost."* *"She certainly sounds wonderful – but what will the cost be exactly?"* said Adam. *"Well,"* said God, *"let's say an arm, a leg and your right ear."*

Despite the promised return, Adam is not at all happy about this. He ponders the arrangement for some time, finally saying, *"I think that's really too much to ask – what would I get for, say, a rib?"*.

And the rest, as they say, is history.

A tough one

Once there was a fairground strongman. During his act, one trick was to take an orange and place it in the crook of his arm. He would then bend his arm and squeeze all the juice out of the orange. Once this was done he would challenge the audience, offering a cash prize to anyone who could get an extra drop out of the mangled orange.

One day, after many people had tried and failed, one apparently unlikely candidate came forward. He was the very opposite of the strongman, but he took his turn, squeezed and squeezed ... and finally succeeded in getting a further drop of orange juice out of the orange.

The strongman and the audience were amazed. The strongman handed over the money and, seeking to discover how this had been possible, he asked what the man did for a living. *"I'm a buyer with the Ford Motor Company,"* he said.

Note: This is the kind of story that can be told linking to an organisation of specific relevance to the group to which it is told. I was told this first in a publishing environment and the company referred to was W. H. Smith (followed by the comment: *"not all buyers are like that ... some are worse."*).

HANG ON A MINUTE

Communicating by telephone

The telephone deserves special mention here. If communication is difficult face to face, how much more difficult must it be when you cannot see someone? Try telling someone to describe how to tie a shoelace, for instance (no demonstrations!); voice-only communications need special care. Even getting through to the correct person can cause problems as this, true, story makes clear:

A visitor is waiting to see someone in an outer office. He chats to the secretary of the person he is visiting. He likes her and they get on so well that he is on the point of asking her out when his host appears and ushers him into the inner office. An hour or so later as he leaves the secretary is not at her desk. Disappointed, he goes back to his car, but after just a few miles decides not to leave it and pulls over to use his mobile telephone. He asks to be put through and nervously, as a voice answers, rushes into his 'pitch': *"We met an hour ago when I visited your boss,"* he gabbled, *"and I wondered if you would come out for a meal with me"*. To his surprise he got an instant *"Yes"*, made an arrangement to meet at a nearby Italian restaurant the following day, and rang off.

The next day he was met in the restaurant by the firm's tealady. She had been wheeling her trolley past the empty desk as the phone rang, and was not about to pass up a free dinner.

(Voicemail machine) **"** *I am sorry. No real people are available at present, please press ...* **"** Overheard

WHAT?

Open questions are best. These, which cannot be answered 'yes' or 'no', are most likely to get people talking, produce real information in reply and create an acceptable style of inquiry for those questioned.

The idea of open questions calls to mind the most elegant statement highlighting this: Rudyard Kipling's poem *The Elephant's Child:*

I keep six honest serving-men
(They taught me all I knew)
Their names are What and Why and When
And How and Where and Who.
I send them over land and sea
I send them east and west;
But after they have worked for me,
I give them all a rest.

I let them rest from nine till five,
For I am busy then,
As well as breakfast, lunch, and tea,
For they are hungry men.
But different folk have different views;

I know a person small –
She keeps ten million serving-men,
Who get no rest at all!
She sends 'em abroad on her own affairs,
From the second she opens her eyes –
One million Hows, two million Wheres,
And seven million Whys!

For some questions there is just no answer:
Why, when you dial a wrong number, is it never engaged?
Why does the partner who snores always go to sleep first?
How did early man ever discover that lobsters were edible?
Why did the first sword swallower do it?
Why is there only one Monopolies Commission?

But such can be useful to enliven a point or to ensure you get an answer to a particular question that can produce a comment.

> **❝** *No question is so difficult to answer as that to which the answer is obvious* **❞** George Bernard Shaw

WHAT A GOOD IDEA

Creativity in business

Managers are, or should be, in the ideas business. More specifically, they are in the business of generating ideas through the way they work and interact with others. They do not have to think of everything themselves, though some managers believe that they do and that others in their team have no ideas at all. They are wrong on both counts.

> 66 *Our minds are like parachutes, only useful when they are open* 99 Alan Margolis

> 66 *Many ideas grow better when transplanted into another mind than the one where they sprang up* 99 Oliver Holmes Jnr

> 66 *What a good idea, Mary, I wonder if one of the men here would like to suggest it* 99 Overheard (at a meeting)

One would never hear such a sexist thing said nowadays of course (I wonder), but I once heard a good, creative response to this sort of thing which took the form of another quote:

> 66 *Whatever women do, they must do twice as well as a man to be thought half as good. Luckily, this is not difficult* 99
> Charlotte Whitton

A definition?

Creativity is a slippery subject, and as the saying has it, 'there is nothing new under the sun'.

The press were crowding around a buxom starlet at a film premiere. She was the sex-goddess of the moment, and was interviewed with the latest of a long line of partners, with whom she was leaving on holiday after the premiere was over. Questions moved from the film, and the part she played, to the new relationship and the man was asked how he felt being with such a fantasy figure (and one, it was hinted, of such experience).

"Well," he said, *"I know what to do, and I like to think I know how to do it. I guess the challenge is to make it interestingly different."*

Maybe 'making things interestingly different' is as good a description of creativity as any.

TOWARDS THE 25 HOUR DAY

Managing the time resource

A brief word (what else?) under this heading. It is said that time is nature's way of keeping everything from happening at once. For most of us time, or the lack of it, is a perpetual problem. Creating good use of time needs constant vigilance and those who succeed best at it differentiate themselves positively from those, of similar ability, who do not.

The problem is largely one of discipline and commitment; those who truly want to be good time managers (and who study the techniques of keeping themselves well organised) tend to succeed. A process that is characterised by a quotation from the classic author G. K. Chesterton, writing about the decline of Christianity in the Western world:

> 66 *The Christian ideal has not been tried and found wanting. It has been found difficult; and left untried* 99

> 66 *They didn't want it good, they wanted it Wednesday* 99
> Robert Heimleur

" Learn to pause – or nothing worthwhile will catch up with you "
Doug Kling

" Do you want this again – or shall I file it? " Overheard

" Next week there can't be any crisis. My schedule is already full " Henry Kissenger

" My manager has a terrible memory – never forgets anything " Overheard

Procrastination will rule - one of these days, OK?

There are probably many stories that can be used to define procrastination (but I have not got round to recording them all yet). However, this is typical:

A man is lying very ill in hospital. The doctors come and go, specialists are sent for, but no clue is discovered as to the cause of his illness. More tests are done, so many that his life becomes a routine: a test one day, the results a week later, then another test and another wait for the result. But still no cause for his sickness is discovered.

Then one Friday a doctor comes in and tells him, *"At last we know what's wrong with you. But I'm afraid there is some bad news – and also some very bad news – which do you want first?".* The man struggles to answer, *"Let's have the bad news,"* he says. *"Well, I'm afraid the test shows that you only have one week to live,"* says the doctor. *"My God,"* says the man, *"in that case, what on earth is the very bad news?"*

The doctor looks embarrassed: *"Well, we got the test result in last Thursday,"* he says, *"er ... but we forgot to tell you".*

And that is certainly procrastination.

WARNING: DO NOT PUT OFF USING THIS STORY – TELL SOMEONE NOW.

NOTE: Even five minutes saved every working day will give you more than two extra days of capacity in a year - see page 89 for additional comment about how things mount up.

Inscrutable yet insightful

I once saw a framed poster in someone's office; it was typical in format of the many, often clichéd, maxims presented in this way.

This one had boldly printed on it in Chinese writing the word 'Crisis'.
It was expressed in the form, not of one, but of the two Chinese characters shown below.

The first represents the word for Chaos. The second signifies the word Opportunity.

Interesting, especially considering the age of the Chinese language – and not a bad way to think about, and perhaps respond to, a crisis!

A facility with numbers

In this sixth — sorry, seventh — section we touch on another core skill.
Everybody knows something about numbers. We know we would like a
cheque for a million pounds, but our facility with numbers often leaves
something to be desired; this is especially true
of big numbers.

Big, mind-bogglingly big

Here is an interesting little teaser you can use to illustrate how people's feel
for numbers is often false. Ask people to draw a line representing a billion:

0

one billion

Then ask them to mark a point on the line that represents a million.
Encourage them to do it quickly to record their immediate impression. Most
people will put such a mark about a quarter, even a third, of the way along
from nought. In fact, as a million (1,000,000) is only one thousandth of a
billion (1,000,000,000), the line should only be a minute distance from the
zero at the left hand end of the line. To all intents and purposes it touches the
end of the line.

How things mount up

This story is told in various guises, but the main point remains the same: it is a complex version of the old proverb that you should 'look after the pennies, and the pounds will look after themselves'.

In ancient Persia a courtier of the King invented the game of chess. The King was so taken with this that he offered him any prize he wanted as a reward. The courtier asked for a grain of wheat for the first square of the chess board, two for the second, four for the third and so on – doubling each time. The courtier was clearly numerate. After ten doublings the total number of grains is over 1000. After doubling for each of the 64 squares on a chessboard this exponential growth produced more grain than had been grown in the history of the world, a number in the quadrillions with eighteen noughts after it.

Similarly, if you put £1000 in the bank at 10% interest, even after a hundred years it would only be worth £11,000. But if you add the ten percent to the principal each year as the hundred years goes by, you end up with £22 million!

Work it out

A classic teaser involving numbers asks what the next number is in the following series of figures:

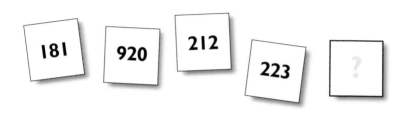

A reminder of the answer is on page 95.

Statistics are a highly logical and precise way of stating half-truths inaccurately NASA document

Lies, damned lies and statistics

Statistics have been called a group of numbers looking for an argument. The heading here is taken from a quotation, usually abbreviated, and attributed to Disraeli:

> *There are three kinds of lies: lies, damned lies and statistics*

And statistics too are often subject to a certain misunderstanding. Statisticians themselves do not help:

> *Statisticians say there are two kinds of people in the world: those that divide people into categories ... and the rest*
> Overheard

> *Too many crooks spoil the percentage* H. Chandler

Boss: "*I can't make head or tail of these figures of yours: half the costs seem to be left out and half the revenue seems not to have materialised. What goes on?*"

Employee: "*Well, to tell you the truth, I was half expecting you to say that.*"

Whatever else you may say about statistics, they can certainly cause confusion. Managers can only operate with certain facts about their nature clear in their minds.

Exploding the figures

George was employed in a multinational and did a great deal of travelling. It was an unavoidable part of his job. But he hated it. Not just the time away and the indifferent hotels; he was scared of flying. His fear intensified during a period of more noticeable terrorist activity. The odds of there being a bomb on a plane were quoted in the newspapers and, although large, he worried still more. His colleagues did their best to reassure him, and during a discussion one of them quoted another statistic: the odds of there being two bombs on one plane were astronomical.

Thereafter he always felt much safer; on subsequent trips he packed a bomb.

The above obviously speaks of the sort of statistical awareness that led to a statistician drowning when wading across a river with an average depth of two feet.

In business, bearing in mind that time is money, it is the financial figures – costs, revenue and ultimately, profits – that are apt to be most important.

66 *Anyone who lives within their means suffers from a lack of imagination* 99 Lionel Stander

66 *Just about the time you think you can make both ends meet, somebody moves the ends* 99 Pansy Penner

66 *It is not a sale until the money's in the bank* 99 Overheard

Asked what the most beautiful words in the English language were, Dorothy Parker is reported to have said:

66 *Cheque enclosed* 99

So, where would we all be without those wonderful people – the accountants – to guide us through the financial jungle?

66 *Accountants are boring, but actuaries are dead boring* 99 Overheard

Simple really ...

The course was a general management programme. One course participant could not get anything right regarding finance and, by the time the course concluded, he was very much the class dunce. As attendees dispersed back to their respective companies the group agreed to meet up a year later to see how everyone was faring. In due course a dinner was arranged at a smart restaurant. The 'dunce' arrived a little late, but as he did so it was clear to all from the Porsche he parked outside, the suit he wore and a dozen other signs of affluence, that he was doing very well for himself.

"I would never have thought it possible," said the course tutor, *"tell us, what are you doing?"* *"It wasn't easy,"* he replied, *"I was laid off by my employer soon after the course finished. I then tried various things without much success, so I finally started up in business myself – in the import/export business in Africa. I discovered that I could buy things for $2 on one side of the border and sell them for $4 on the other. It's gone well, I'm still amazed at how that 2 per cent adds up."*

Maybe understanding outcomes is more important than understanding the theory.

The answer to the numbers teaser on page 90 is 242 (because it is simply the numbers 18, 19, 20 etc. written to overlap the line)

A CHANGE IS AS GOOD AS A REST

Coping with change

We live in dynamic times. Much that goes on in management is concerned with change. Managers must decide whether change is necessary, when it may be necessary, what must be done and how it can be made to work. Change is good, of course. Everyone is in favour of change ... right up to the moment that someone comes into their office and says, *"There are going to be some changes here!"*.

Some may define change as what other people must do.

66 *You can't sit on the lid of progress. If you do you will be blown to pieces* 99 Henry Kaiser

66 *When you're through changing, you're through. Change is a process, not a goal; a journey, not a destination* 99 Robert Kriegal and David Brant

The fable elephant and the giraffe

Once upon a time there was a giraffe who built himself a special house. It had tall doorways and high ceilings. The corridors were narrow so that space went into the living areas and every detail was just right. His family loved it, they planted roses round the door – climbing ones – and reckoned it was the best home for giraffes ever built.

The giraffe invited his friend the elephant in to see. But when the elephant got to the door he didn't fit – he was stuck outside.

The giraffe was able to help. The door had been made adjustable and he

Continued ...

explained that it was easy to expand the width and did just that. The elephant came in, and immediately the telephone rang. The giraffe excused himself and rushed to answer it. "*Make yourself at home,*" he cried as he ran from the room.

The elephant was soon having problems. He sat down but broke the chair. He tried to follow the giraffe upstairs but got jammed and broke the banisters. When his friend returned he apologised, and the giraffe said, "*No problem, I'll enroll you in keep fit classes so that it is no problem on future visits.*"

The elephant was unconvinced and left saying that he could never visit such a house again.

Moral: the giraffe is the main player, the environment he has created is his and he is in charge. Despite their friendship and things in common, the elephant will always be the outsider – changes are needed, but who should change what?

Some trainers use the descriptions 'elephant' and 'giraffe' to link to similar situations as people attempt to work together in organisations.

When change comes ... s-l-o-w-l-y

It is an oft-used phrase that we should 'not keep reinventing the wheel', but one can look further back:

The wheel was not invented in a flash of creative brilliance; like everything else it initially had certain bugs and these took time to sort out. The very first wheels, the product of the innovative Kwik-trip Korporation, were in fact square in shape. They did beat carrying heavy things, but only just – and they gave a somewhat bumpy ride. Customers bought them, or rather, exchanged them as money hadn't been invented yet, but they also complained. Ug, who was in charge of new product development at KK, thought long and hard about possible changes. Then he had an idea.

He set to work and made a new batch of wheels incorporating his idea. When one of his best customers arrived a few days later he proudly showed off his latest innovation. *"A change for the better,"* said Ug, but his customer was not immediately enthusiastic. *"How on earth is that better?"* he said, *"it's triangular!"*.

"That's right!" he was told enthusiastically, *"one less bump!"*.

THIS IS IT!

Love it or hate it, we all have to cope with it. With some exceptions, we know that:

> *If your system works well, it must be obsolete* Anon

> *Leaving it in the box means you don't have to pack it up when the new one arrives* Anon

A rhyme relevant here is:

I bought the latest computer;
It came completely loaded.
It was guaranteed for 90 days,
But in 30 was outmoded.

Nothing, but nothing, moves as fast as the pace of technology.

Faster, more accurate – more certain?

Many of us also know not only that we will never be experts, but that we will always be vulnerable.

Thus:

If a packet hits a pocket on socket on a port,
And the bus is interrupted as a very last resort,
And the address of the memory makes your floppy disk abort,
Then the socket packet pocket has an error to report.

If your cursor finds a menu item followed by a dash,
And the double-clicking icon puts your window in the trash,
And your data is corrupted 'cause the index doesn't hash,
Then your situation's hopeless and your system's going to crash.

Unless, of course, you are an expert.

Definition: *The word 'Expert' is derived from two root words –*
'Ex', which is a has-been, and 'Spurt', which is a drip under pressure

> *The words 'out of sight, out of mind' when translated into Russian by computer were rendered as 'invisible maniac'* Anon

Maybe one day the machines will take over.

> *Sometime in the next thirty years, very quietly one day we will cease to be the brightest thing on Earth*

James McAlear (in the book Visions, published in 1998) – watch this space.

THE ULTIMATE GOAL

A measure of success

> *" If anything goes bad, I did it.*
> *If anything goes semi-bad, then we did it.*
> *If anything goes real good, then you did it "* Bear Brown

Success comes in various forms: from the achievement of targeted results within the organisation to the rewards that achieving them bring to the individual. Most managers recognise this and are careful not to 'confuse activity with achievement', as they say, though a bureaucratic approach can so easily stifle success:

How many bureaucratic managers does it take to change a lightbulb?
Two – one to assure people that everything possible is being done, and one to screw the new bulb into the water tap

Success is most often the result of working at it.

> *" There is no shortcut to any place worth going "* Beverly Sills

Success is a state of mind

The following incident, which occurred as I was waiting to appear on LBC (the London independent talk radio station), illustrates both optimism and positive thinking.

Waiting for my turn (on an item about small business), I started talking to another interviewee. He was there to comment on some technical issue, momentarily in the news, connected to the environment. I asked him if he headed up the technical department. *"No,"* he replied, *"but I aim to."*

I quizzed him further. It transpired that cultivating himself as the organisation's expert with the media was just part of his strategy to enhance his profile within the organisation and make his promotion more likely. Any number of people from the department might have been interviewed for radio. However he had volunteered (assertively, I fancy), done some research and preparation to make sure it went well (sensible: a brief radio interview demands a very particular style of communication) and made a good job of his first appearance.

This time they had asked for him individually. I do not know what he is doing now – but I would bet he is thriving.

> 66 *Success is not the result of spontaneous combustion. You must first set yourself on fire* 99
> Fred Shiro

Success? ... but not for all.

In a large organisation a manager gathers the staff of his section for a briefing. Things have not been going too well: corporate profits are down, a hostile takeover is rumoured, demands for increased productivity abound. Paperwork and hours worked are the only things that seem to be increasing. As they gather for the meeting, people are feeling apprehensive.

The manager opens the proceedings: *"I have good news and bad news,"* says the manager, *"which do you want to hear first?"*. After hasty mutterings amongst themselves the group opt for hearing the bad news first.

"Right," says the manager, *"because of recent problems, the organisation is downsizing. As a result, half of you will not be here tomorrow and the half that does remain must take a cut in salary."* A slide appears identifying two lists of names. There is shock and horror on every face. After what seems a long silence, one of the group asks: *"And what's the good news?"*.

The manger smiles broadly, *"I've been appointed to the Board!"* he says.

———————————— ■ ————————————

> *If at first you do succeed – try to hide your astonishment* Anon

THE ULTIMATE GOAL

When push comes to shove ......

A memo to the boss:

Memorandum

To: John Smith, Divisional Director
From: Mary Peters, Section Head

Weekly Report

I am afraid I must report that this has not been a good week. Problems have included:

- A mistake leading to a computerised database being irretrievably deleted; work to reinstate it will take at least a month

- Three people out of the team strength of eight being absent throughout the week, I suspect for no good reason

- Susan, my new secretary, announcing that she is pregnant; her departure to have the baby will coincide with our peak season and she has been in position just long enough for maternity benefit to be due. (George has asked for a transfer, and I suspect there is a connection – anyway he will need to be replaced)

- Personnel have brought forward all staff appraisals so that they clash with next month's reorganisation

- I received a letter about the computer clerk you insisted I sacked last month; she is taking her case to an industrial tribunal

Actually none of the foregoing is true, though I do plan to transfer George if I can prise him and Susan apart for long enough, before there really are costly consequences.

I just wanted you to keep the fact that productivity was 1 percent down last week in perspective. We will make it up and in any case, as you can see, things could be worse.

THE ULTIMATE GOAL

I am not sure that I would recommend this as an approach. The point remains, however: we will none of us be unfailingly successful all the time, but the balance must be positive. Perhaps success is best regarded as being an above average rate of strike. Besides, even when you do succeed, the likelihood is that no one will notice:

> 66 *Doing something well in my company is like wetting yourself in a dark blue suit. It gives you a nice warm feeling, but no one else notices* 99 Overheard

> 66 *Calamities are of two kinds: misfortunes to ourselves, and good fortune to others* 99 Ambrose Bierce

> 66 *When sorrows come, they come not in single spies, but in battalions!* 99 William Shakespeare

> 66 *The man who makes no mistakes does not make anything* 99 Edward John Phelps

> 66 *In my company we are so confused, we are stabbing each other in the chest* 99 Overheard

If all else fails .....

If success eludes you and all your personal attempts to achieve are dogged by failure then you clearly need to hire a consultant.

Definition: *1: A consultant is someone who has their arm round your shoulder, their tongue in your ear, their hand in your pocket and their faith in your gullibility*

Definition: *2: A consultant is someone who borrows your watch to tell you the time; and then keeps the watch*

Finally here, remember that although:

> *St George's victory may have been due as much to the fact that dragons don't like tinned meat as to his skill as a swordsman* Anon

you should never rely on luck to achieve success.

> *Luck is only useful to explain why other people succeed; especially those you dislike* Anon

All help gratefully received

Business (and training) is, for the most part, not a solo effort. The intention is that this book will help, either directly or by prompting your own thinking, to refresh all parts of your presentations and training. That said, we will end with a story about help.

A businessman is invited to speak at the dinner following a major conference. He is flattered to be asked and, despite a hectic schedule, agrees and puts it in his diary. On the day of the event his wife helps him pack. The function is black tie and far enough away that he must change at the hotel where it will take place.

After a busy day, he arrives at the hotel with little time to spare and rushes to his room to change. With the minutes ticking by he finds that the bow tie in his case is real, not the one on elastic he usually wears. It needs tying in a bow and he cannot remember how. As he struggles to get it right, he calls room service hoping for assistance, but the chambermaid who comes to his room does not know how to do it.

Desperate and with minutes to go before he must address the expectant group downstairs, he remembers he has heard sounds in the room next door. He risks knocking on the door. A man opens the door and he explains his dilemma, asking if the man can tie the tie for him. *"Yes, come in,"* he is told. He enters the room and is told to lie down on the bed. Now worried, and thinking he has chanced across an axe murderer, or worse, he remembers the time and the importance of the occasion and does as he is told. The man lifts up his head, threads the tie round his neck and knots a perfect bow.

Delighted, he backs towards the door mumbling his thanks, but cannot resist taking a moment to ask, *"Why did you get me to lie on the bed?"*. *"I'm an undertaker,"* comes the reply, *"and I've never done it on a body that stood up."*

There are many circumstances where help is welcome. But it may not always come from obvious sources or in obvious ways.

ABOUT THE AUTHOR

Patrick Forsyth is a marketing consultant and trainer. He also writes extensively on business matters (*I love being a writer. What I can't stand is the paperwork – Peter De Vries*): on marketing, sales and a variety of communications management skills including training: *Running an Effective Training Session, Gower Publishing.*

Patrick began his career on the editorial side of publishing (*As repressed sadists are said to become policemen or butchers, so those with an irrational fear of life become publishers – Cyril Connolly*), soon moving to the sales, publicity and marketing of books (*If a book is worth reading, it is worth buying – John Ruskin*). He then joined a management institute, and from there moved into consultancy and training (*He who can does. He who cannot, teaches – George Bernard Shaw*). In 1990 he started his own firm, Touchstone Training & Consultancy. He undertakes training in many forms: public seminars, for organisations such as the Institute of Management, tailored in-company programmes for clients in a variety of industries, even individual tutorials. His work also regularly takes him overseas .

In addition to books, which he says he writes, *"as a kind of revenge on the publishing industry for not making me Managing Director in my first six months there,"* he writes articles and training materials: for example creating support material for multimedia training in the form of audio and video packages etc. (*Etc is a symbol used to make others think we know more than we do – Anon*).

Patrick is the author of three further Management Pocketbooks titles, on meetings, negotiation and selling (*There is a good saying to the effect that when a new book appears one should read an old one – Winston Churchill*), see page 121.

Contact

You can contact Patrick at:

Touchstone Training & Consultancy

28 Saltcote Maltings

Heybridge, Maldon

Essex CM9 4QP

Telephone/fax: 01621-859300

Or: E-mail: patrick@touchstonetc.freeserve.co.uk

" I would never read a book if it were possible to talk half an hour with the man who wrote it " Woodrow Wilson

ACKNOWLEDGEMENTS

> ❝ *If you steal from one author, it's plagiarism;*
> *if you steal from many, its research* ❞ Wilson Mizner

> ❝ *Misquotation is, in fact, the pride and privilege of the learned.*
> *A widely read man never quotes accurately, for the obvious reason*
> *that he has read too widely* ❞ Hesketh Pearson

In compiling this book, I racked my brains, wrote a few pages, and then realised I needed assistance and contacted a number of friends, colleagues, associates and sundry contacts. Some I know and collaborate with now, others are contacts from the past. Most of those I contacted were helpful, some replied at length, and their replies both reminded me of things long forgotten and added to my fund of 'quotables' in all the categories used in the book. So thanks are due to all.

Unable to promise financial reward, I promised instead the visibility — notoriety? - which comes from being in print in the unique Pocketbook format, in a book which the publishers assure me will sell in its thousands. I gladly mention here, therefore, all those who helped and whose contributions are quoted or tweaked in some way to include them here.

So, (in A – Z order) my thanks go to:

Kathy Bailey, Robin Birn, Rod Davey, Fiona Dent, David Horchover, Peter Kirkby, David Martin, Peter O'Riley, David Senton, Diane Watson, and Pat Wellington.

Those others who did not respond to my request no doubt had the following in mind:

> 66 *A friend in need is a friend to be avoided* 99 Lord Samuel

Having completed this book, I will now attempt successfully to remember the content presented here to assist my own training and other work. I resolve also to bolster my imperfect memory by recording any additions I come across more systematically in the future than I have done in the past.

Which reminds me, with only the loosest of links to failing memory, of the definition of getting old.

Definition: *You know you are getting old not, in fact, when you pause halfway up the stairs and wonder what you were going up for. Rather it is when you pause halfway up the stairs, wonder what you were going up for – and then reconsider further, asking yourself, "Was I going up, or coming down?"*

I like quoting this, though I do not remember why. Now, what comes next?

FUTURE CONTRIBUTION

(The Future) *❝ That period of time in which our affairs prosper, our friends are true and our happiness is assured ❞*
Ambrose Bierce

I hope that you have enjoyed this book and found it useful.

In the confident expectation that it will go into an early reprint, fourteen foreign languages and that *Hook Your Audience II* will be a must for the publisher, perhaps I may end by suggesting that, if you have any pet potential entries that you feel any future edition would be bereft without, you send them to me for consideration. Any that are collected in this way and which are subsequently used will, of course, be acknowledged and contributors will receive a copy of any new edition that includes their suggestion.

Make a note now on the following page, then please send any ideas to the address shown on page 117.

❝ Help someone when they are in trouble and they will remember you when they are in trouble again ❞ Overheard

ADDITIONAL THOUGHTS

Space is provided here to note additional examples of useful material.

_____

_____

_____

_____

_____

_____

_____

_____

_____

_____

Order Form

Name

Position

Company

Address

Telephone

Facsimile

E-mail

VAT No.
(EC companies)

Your
Order Ref

Please send me: No. copies ▼

Hook Your Audience

The   Pocketbook

The   Pocketbook

The   Pocketbook

The   Pocketbook

Order by Post

Management Pocketbooks Ltd
14 East Street, Alresford, Hampshire SO24 9EE UK

Order by Phone, Fax or Internet

Tel: +44 (0)1962 735573
Fax: +44 (0)1962 733637
E-mail: pocketbks@aol.com
Web: www.pocketbook.co.uk

MANAGEMENT
POCKETBOOKS

Customers in USA should contact:

Stylus Publishing, LLC
22883 Quicksilver Drive, Sterling, VA 20166-2012
Telephone: 703 661 1581 or 800 232 0223
Facsimile: 703 661 1501 E-mail: styluspub@aol.com

The Management Pocketbook Series

FINALLY

At the end of the day, when push comes to shove, remember that while business is a serious business, doing business and being in business can be – perhaps should be – fun.

As Samuel Butler said:

> 66 *The one serious conviction that a man should have is that nothing is to be taken too seriously* 99

Note: The erratum below is slightly tweaked from a quotation attributed to Alisdair Gray. Keep on quoting – meantime this must be the last page.

ERRATUM

This note has been included by mistake.

Once I couldn't finish anything but now